This book belongs to

and no one else!

(I'm serious.)

Balzer + Bray is an imprint of HarperCollins Publishers.

You-niquely You: An Emmie & Friends Interactive Journal
Copyright © 2020 by Terri Libenson

ISBN 978-0-06-299838-5

Typography by Terri Libenson and Laura Mock
21 22 23 24 SCP 10 9 8 7 6 5 4 3 2

First Edition

YOU-NIQUELY
you

your drawing
of YOU

GAH-geous!

EMMIE

List the **BEST** things about YOU:

✓ I'm creative.

✓ I'm funny.(well that's what my friends say)

✓ I'm good at skelething

✓ I'm good at skipping

✓ I've got a good imagination.

✓ I love action movies.

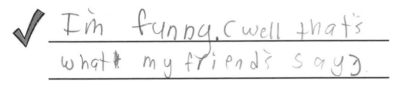

Practice some secret messages here:

Now decode some of mine!

TYLER ROSS HAS THE CUTEST FRECKLE.

I HHAAATE GYM

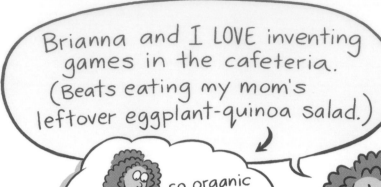

Brianna and I LOVE inventing games in the cafeteria. (Beats eating my mom's leftover eggplant-quinoa salad.)

so organic it moved

Here are a bunch of our games:

spork sculpting

glue

Inventing hybrid utensils

whiskula knorf

stradle

food tray Jenga

Grossology challenge (combining disgusting ingredients)

just ate pizza cheese and mayo

I love to express myself through art, like drawing comics. I can even make myself the star.

You try!

Anything goes!

Here are some ideas to help you start:

★ Make a comic about funny things your pet does.

★ Make a comic about a cause you believe in.

★ Make a comic about your quirky family.

★ Make a comic about you as a hero.

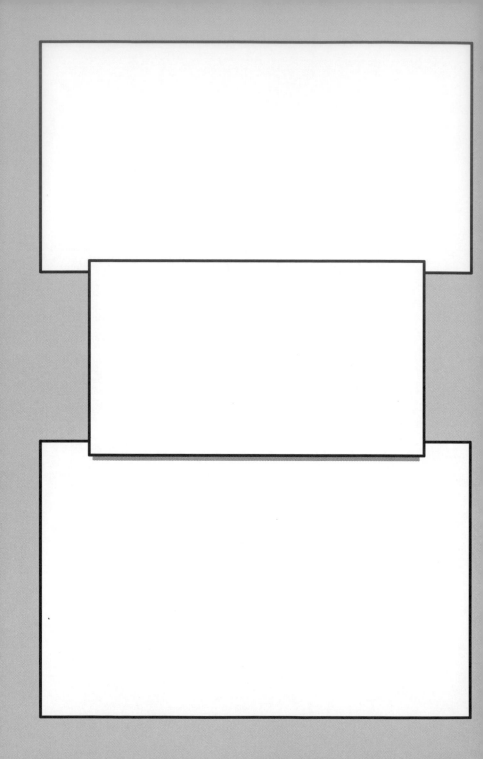

Dear 18-year-old ___Taylor___,
(your name)
___I hope that i am___
___successful and___
_____
_____
_____
_____
_____
_____
_____
_____
_____
_____
_____
_____
_____
_____
_____
_____
_____
_____
_____

Sincerely,
_____-year-old _____
(your age
now) (your name)

What are the strangest foods you've eaten? Draw them here.

Once I did something embarrassing, and thought it was the worst day...

crying in bathroom

...until it became the best!

I made some new friends. You'll never guess how....

describing the outcome

What was your most embarrassing event? Draw or write it here:

Did it turn out okay?
☐ yes (whew) ☑ no (dang)

What would YOU choose as your superpower? Draw it here.

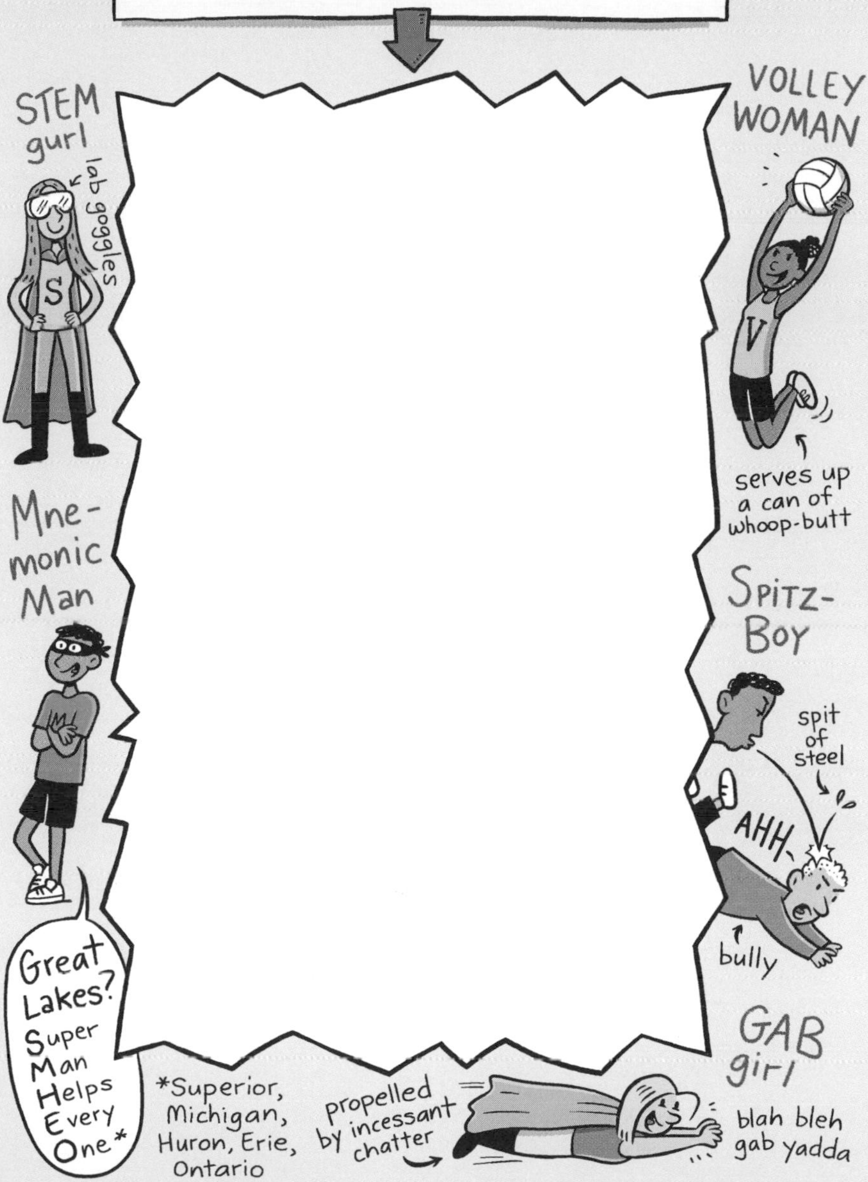

My very, very, VERY favorite class is (you guessed it) **art**.

My least favorite is gym.

BONK

List YOURS here:

Favorite class: _____

Least favorite: _____

List some made-up classes you WISH you could take:

_____

_____

_____

_____

_____

_____

MINE:

This is the phone my parents made me use for most of seventh grade — **UGH!**

antenna

screen the size of postage stamp

key pad (#s and letters on same buttons

arrow scroller thingy

My dream phone would be... well... a <u>regular</u> phone.

BUT it would have some really unusual features:

keyboard that autocorrects awkwardness

camera that makes me look like a movie star

fully waterproof ('cause I'd drop it in paint water)

mind-reading app (for Tyler Ross)

If your phone had supercool features, what would they be? Label 'em here:

Having a crush can be *haaard.*

dreamboat

An icebreaker might make it easier to talk to your crush.

Here are some of my best* pickup lines to lure 'em!

✓ Are you a broom? 'Cause you swept me off my feet.

✓ Your hand looks heavy. Want me to hold it? ★

✓ Brace yourself**... I like you.

✓ If you were a veggie, you'd be a cute-cumber.

I'm in a love pickle

* according to best friend. Have yet to be tested on actual crush.

** only works on those with braces. Duh.

Now make up your own lines!

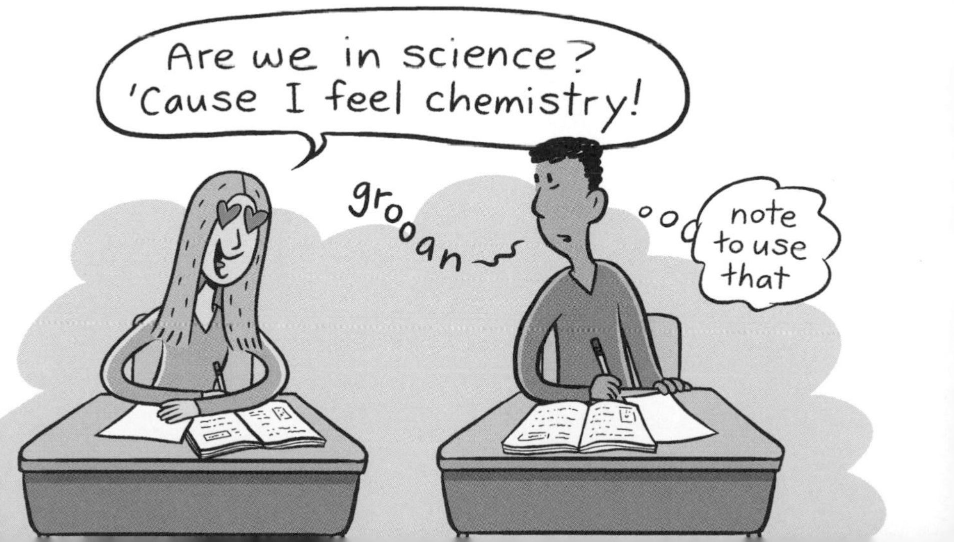

My favorite trip *ever* was to Chicago. Here are some memories.

Millennium Park

big shiny bean

Paul Klee painting

Art Institute of Chicago

deep, deep, deep dish

ew.

Chicago-style pizza! (which my dad hates)

Did you ever go on a trip you loved?

Where was it? _____

_____

When? _____

_____

What kind of things did you do?

_____
_____
_____

What kind of food did you eat?

_____
_____
_____

What were your favorite sights to see?

_____
_____
_____

What was the best part of the trip?

_____
_____
_____

The worst?

_____
_____

BRI

For example, if he wants to memorize a word for a spelling bee, he'll make up something like this.

Grace's
Elegant
Old
Grandpa
Rode
A
Pig
Home
Yesterday

har!

*called "mnemonics"

Can you make up some mnemonics for these?

SATURN!

S _____
A _____
T _____
U _____
R _____
N _____

THEATER!

T _____
H _____
E _____
A _____
T _____
E _____
R _____

PALETTE!

P _____
A _____
L _____
E _____
T _____
T _____
E _____

FASHION!

ooh la la!

F _____
A _____
S _____
H _____
I _____
O _____
N _____

Show me where you and your friends hang out.

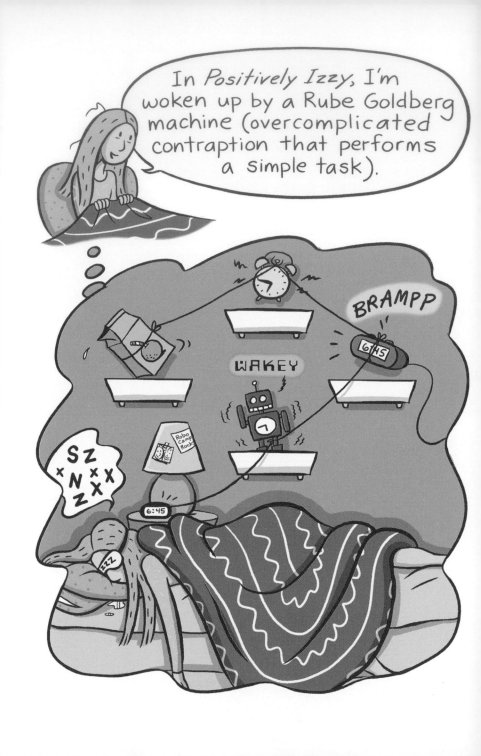

Invent your OWN Rube Goldberg machine! Some ideas for a task:
✔ turn off a light   ✔ brush teeth
   ✔ pour cereal in a bowl
✔ clean your room (I need that!)

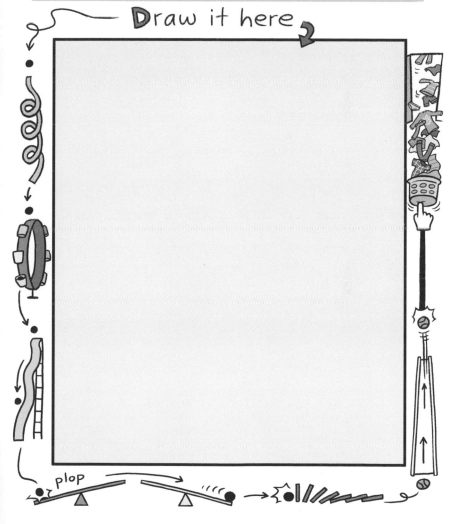

Draw it here

plop

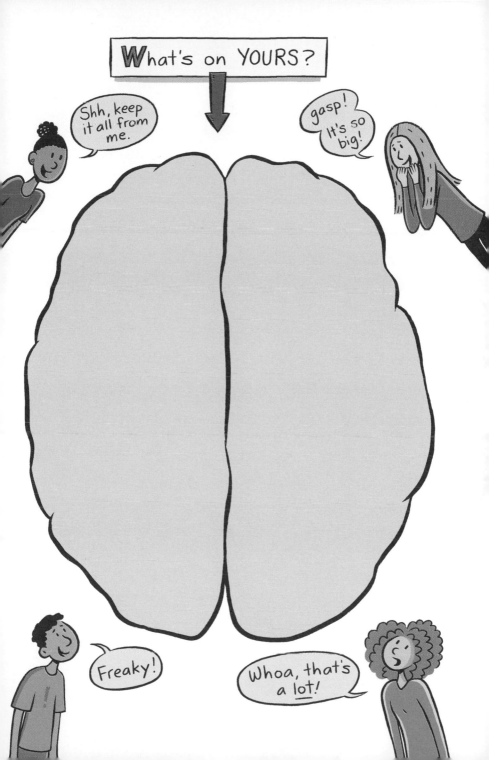

If you know me, you know I <u>hate</u> being onstage.

But if I'm gonna be here, I might as well have a good stage name.*

eek!

★ FIND YOURS! ★

First letter of first name		First letter of last name	
A Brynn	**N** Harley	**A** Oz	**N** Valentine
B Lord	**O** South	**B** Havoc	**O** Mercury
C Jet	**P** Muse	**C** Wilde	**P** Nova
D Cash	**Q** Phoenix	**D** Vicious	**Q** Lightning
E Coco	**R** Sky	**E** Bones	**R** Keys
F Cage	**S** Justice	**F** Gaga	**S** Winter
G Angel	**T** Moon	**G** Crash	**T** Manchester
H Barron	**U** Brooks	**H** Bravo	**U** Northwest
I Skylarr	**V** Blue	**I** Drake	**V** Barrymore
J Sunshine	**W** Hawk	**J** Tempest	**W** Quest
K Jade	**X** Quinn	**K** Fame	**X** Buttons
L Red	**Y** Ivy	**L** Starr	**Y** Sparkle
M River	**Z** Cat	**M** Neptune	**Z** Bear

*Mine is Lord Vicious!

I also love <u>ice cream.</u>
(C'mon, who doesn't?)

Some people enjoy
unusual flavors
(not me).

Circle the flavors
you like and cross out
the ones you don't:

chocolate   peanut butter   kale   vanilla   chocolate chip

Rocky Road   Cookies & Cream   lobster   straw-berry   Cheeto dust

Your turn! Draw your family
(or your friends if they're your family.)

FAVORITE THINGS!

I love [book], Camp Robo [robot], [pizza], [ice cream], and [face].

Draw YOUR favorite things.

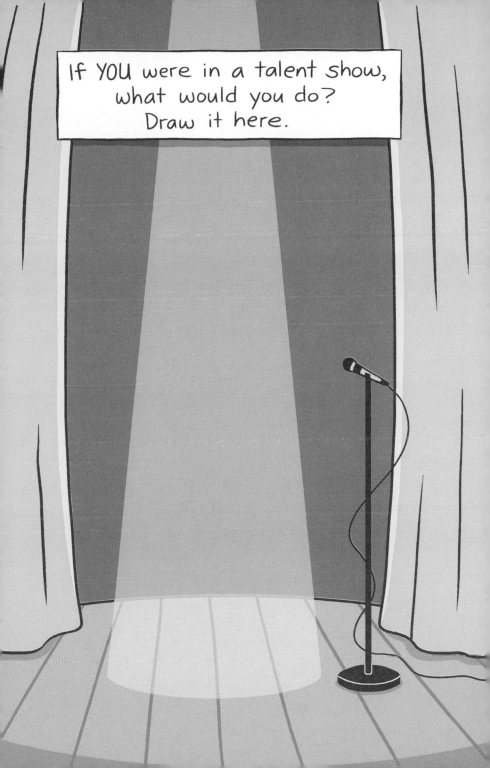

I hate being labeled The Brain. It's 'cause I'm so much more!

I'm also:

| A loyal friend | Future scientist/ inventor | Rom-com buff (surprise!) |

Rosie
↓
ZIP

sob

Is there something YOU'RE known for?

_____

_____

Are there other things you'd LIKE to be known for?

_____

_____

_____

YAY! You're more than a label!

Let's get back to the talent show.

When I performed, I was WAY out of my comfort zone.

But I'm glad I went for it.

CLAP CLAP

Have you ever done anything outside of YOUR comfort zone?

(ex: zip-lining when you're afraid of heights; trying out for a sport when you're an injury magnet)

Explain here

BONK

List all the things on YOUR bucket list:

JAIME

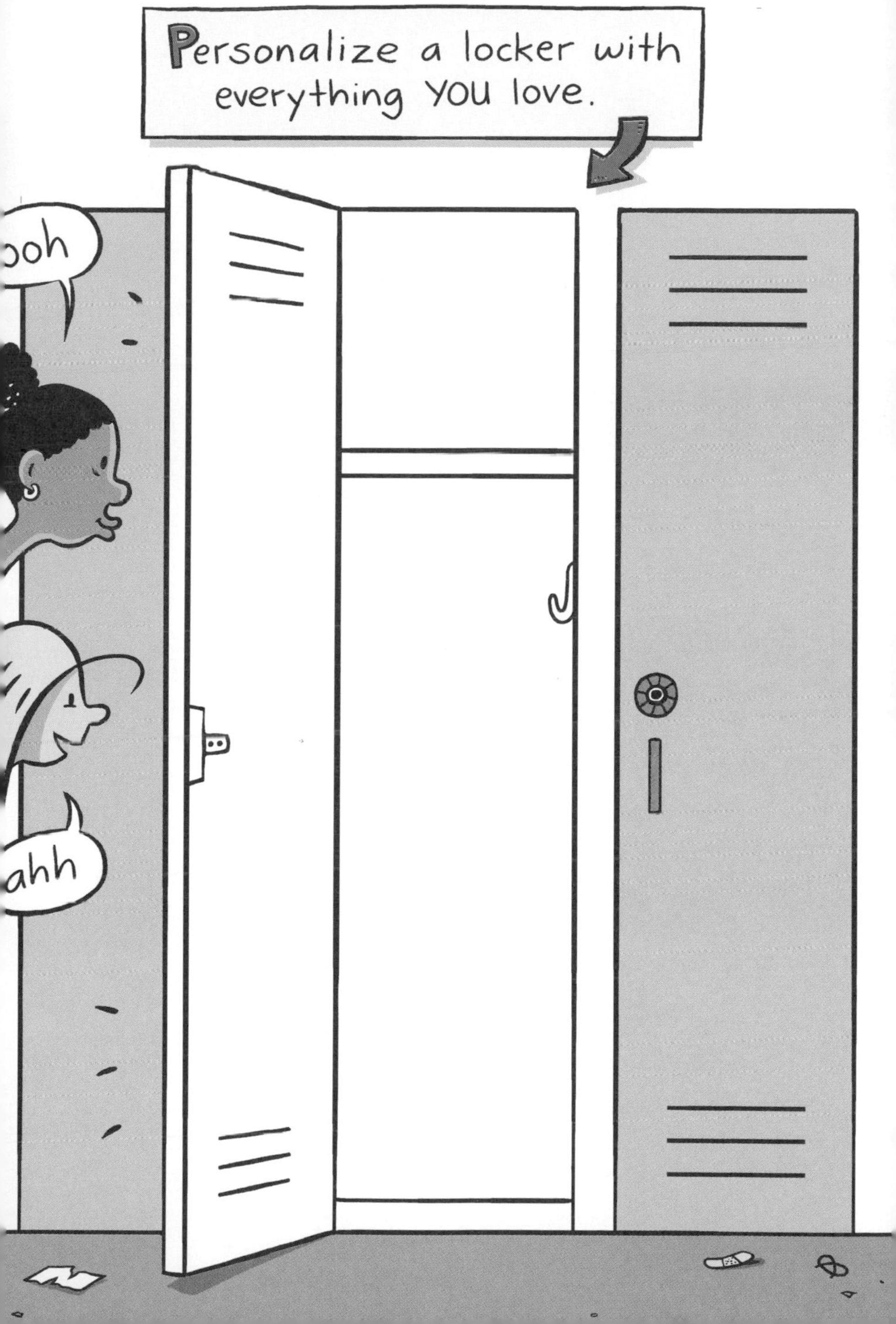
Personalize a locker with everything YOU love.
ooh
ahh

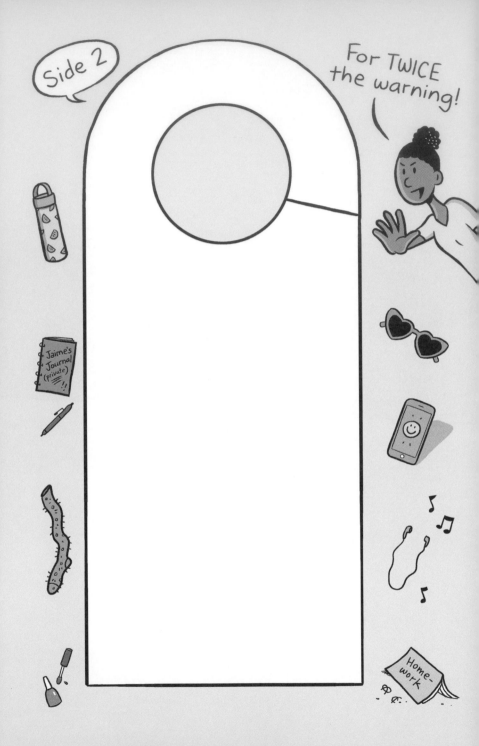

Use my emoji feelings chart!
Point to how you feel today.

(Me? I've already
gone through five
different ones!)

Today I feel:

Any feelings NOT on the chart?
Draw 'em here.

I LOOOVE sleepovers!

They involve all my favorite things: talking, movies, manis, and lots of JUNK FOOD!

I especially love sleepover games, like these:

✓ silliest PJs contest

✓ blindfold makeover — ew — ha ha

✓ indoor glamping — glamour tent

✓ pillowcase decorating — tie-dyed

Make up your own sleepover games!

_____
_____
_____
_____
_____
_____
_____
_____
_____
_____
_____
_____
_____
_____
_____
_____
_____
_____
_____
_____

← custom picture frames
(take a pic of you & your friends
for this!)

"Bad Talent Show"

Here's one.

What do you call a fish with no eyes?

A fsh.

PJ runway

Truth!

TRUTH or DARE

Dare!

When I was really down, I had some great grown-ups by my side.

my mom

Madame Z
(French teacher)

Draw YOUR favorite adult(s) and label everything you love about them:

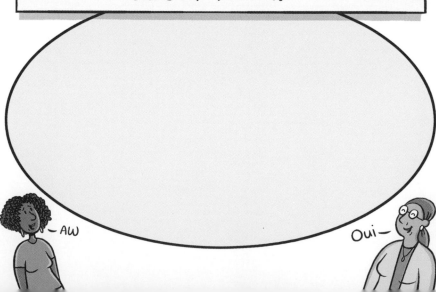

— AW

Oui—

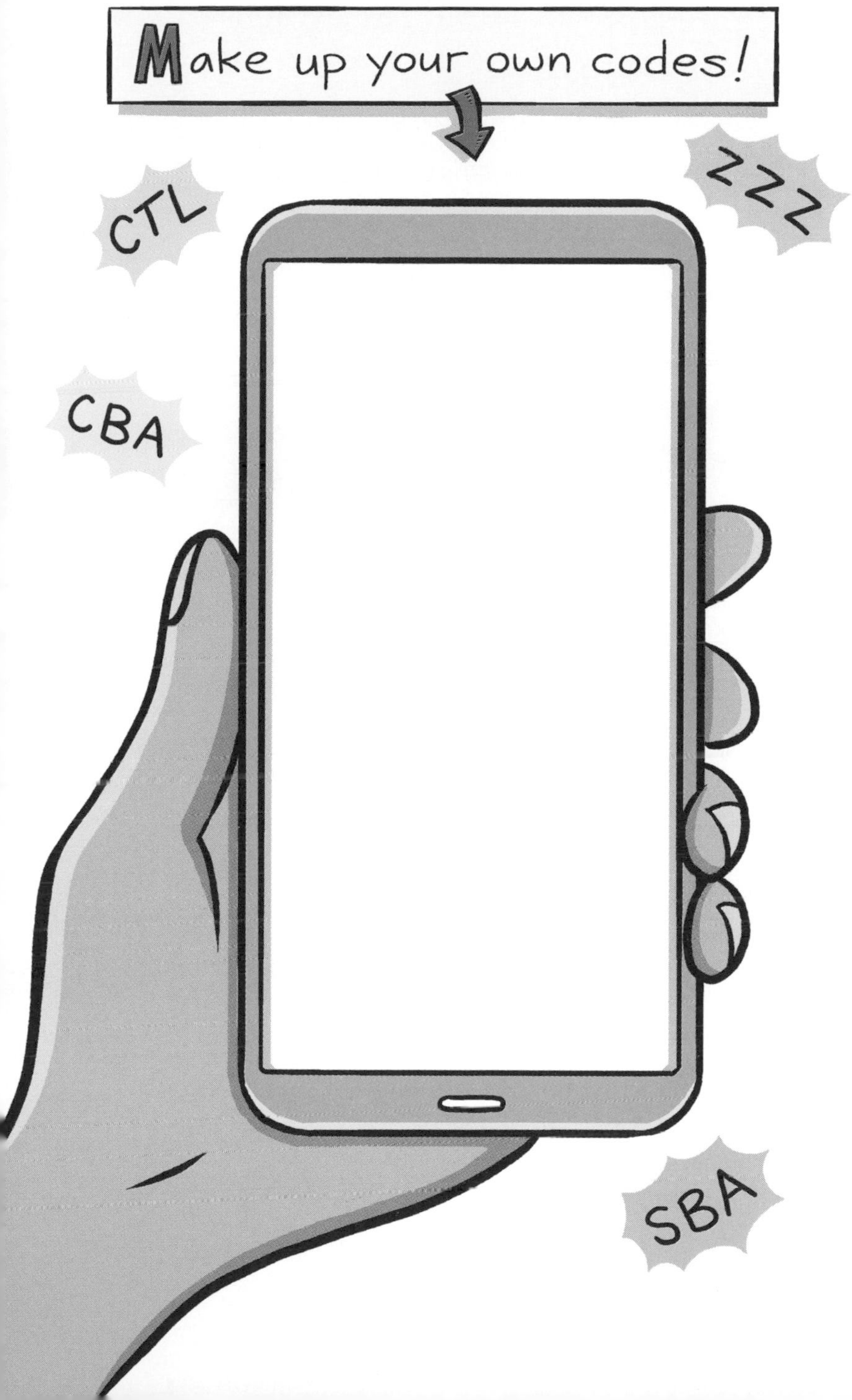
Make up your own codes!
CTL
ZZZ
CBA
SBA

I once took a ride in an inflatable ball. It was stupid fun...

wheeeeeeee

bouncy   bouncy

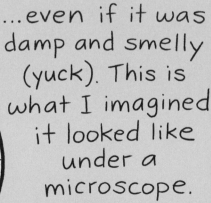

...even if it was damp and smelly (yuck). This is what I imagined it looked like under a microscope.

Take the grossest, smelliest thing or place YOU can think of (your brother's gym sock?) and put it under a microscope.

What kind of creatures would you see?

gross

Name some of YOUR biggest accomplishments:

✓ _____

_____

✓ _____

_____

✓ _____

_____

What else would you LIKE to accomplish?

_____

_____

_____

_____

_____

What kinds of ways would YOU start a new school year?

List some new things you would do. (examples: try harder at math, include the new kid, try the cafeteria "kale bowl")

_____

_____

_____

_____

List things you WOULDN'T do. (examples: send dumb love texts to your crush, worry so much about fitting in, pop that forehead zit)

_____

_____

_____

_____

_____

Write your letters HERE:

cut page here

(FRONT)

cut page here

(BACK)

cut page here

(FRONT)

cut page here

(BACK)

A Personality Quiz!!

Who are you most like?

Are you an EMMIE, a BRI, a JAIME, or a JOE LUNGO (boo)?

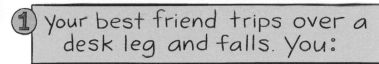

(1) Your best friend trips over a desk leg and falls. You:

A. Make sure they're okay and get the nurse.
B. Sit with them and sympathize.
C. Tell them jokes until they crack up and forget their embarrassment.
D. Point and laugh.

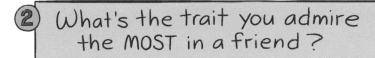

(2) What's the trait you admire the MOST in a friend?

A. A no-nonsense, down-to-earth personality.
B. Sensitivity and a listening ear.
C. A fun-loving, positive attitude.
D. The ability to take a prank.

3 You do awfully on a test. How do you react?

A. "I'm never getting into college!"
B. "Ugh! But this is definitely not my best subject."
C. "Rats. Next time I'll grab a study buddy."
D. "What test?"

4 Your locker is: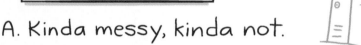

A. Kinda messy, kinda not.
B. A train wreck.
C. Decked out in every trendy locker accessory known to humankind.
D. Smelly, dark, missing all my books.

5 Your texting style is:

A. Short-n-sweet.
B. Lengthy, 'cause it's easier to write than talk.
C. Mostly emojis.
D. Devoid of grammar and sense.

6 Rumor has it the school bully is after you. You:

A. Try and talk some sense into them.
B. Duck-n-dodge.
C. Sweet-talk 'em.
D. I am the school bully.

7 What do you think your future career will be?

A. Scientist or doctor.
B. Something in the arts.
C. Teacher or life coach. Maybe both!
D. Something in the dark arts.

8 The talent show is happening and you're in it! What's your role?

A. Nothing! Not my thing.
B. Stagehand or set designer.
C. Front and center, knocking 'em dead.
D. Hiding behind the curtain, waiting to trip the performer.

9 What would most likely be decorating your school folder?

A. Science stickers.
B. Artsy Sharpie doodles.  best-teas
C. Funny messages between me and my bff.
D. A dent from someone's head.

10 Which Harry Potter character do you most relate to?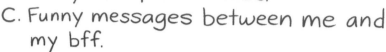

A. Hermione Granger
B. Neville Longbottom
C. The Weasley Twins
D. Lord Voldemort

SCORE

| Mostly As: | You're a BRI! 🙂
You're smart, curious, and enjoy learning.

| Mostly Bs: | You're an EMMIE! 👧
You're artistic, sensitive, and sympathetic.

| Mostly Cs: | You're a JAIME! 🧒
You're friendly, fun-loving, and enjoy people.

| Mostly Ds: | You're a JOE! 👴
You're evil and awful. But good news — you can still change your ways. START NOW!

_____TGYloc_____'s JOURNAL

starts here.

well i kinda just go back
from my party

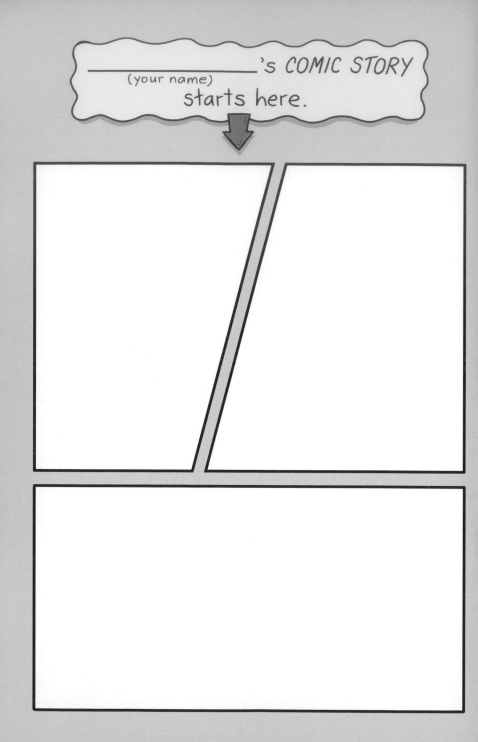
_____'s COMIC STORY

(your name)

starts here.

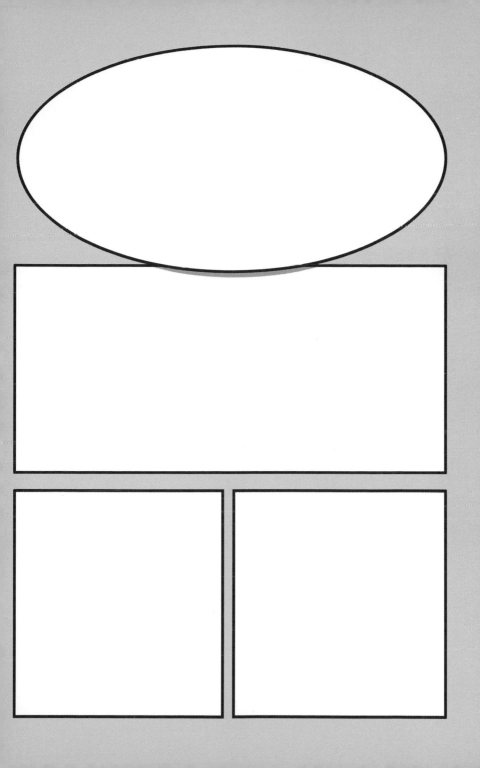

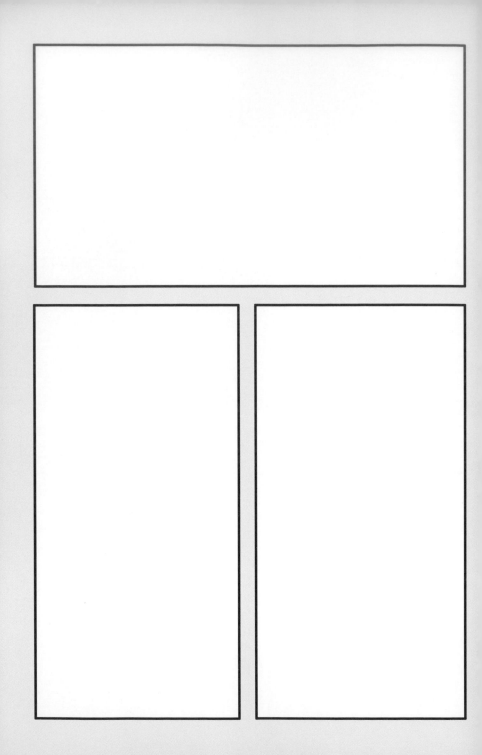

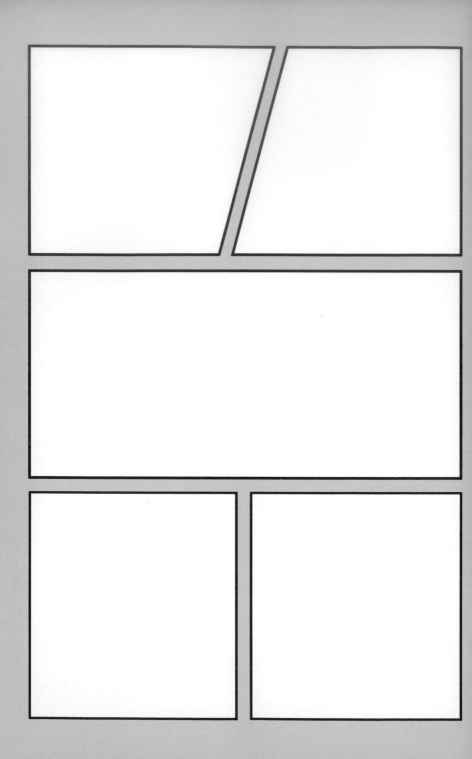

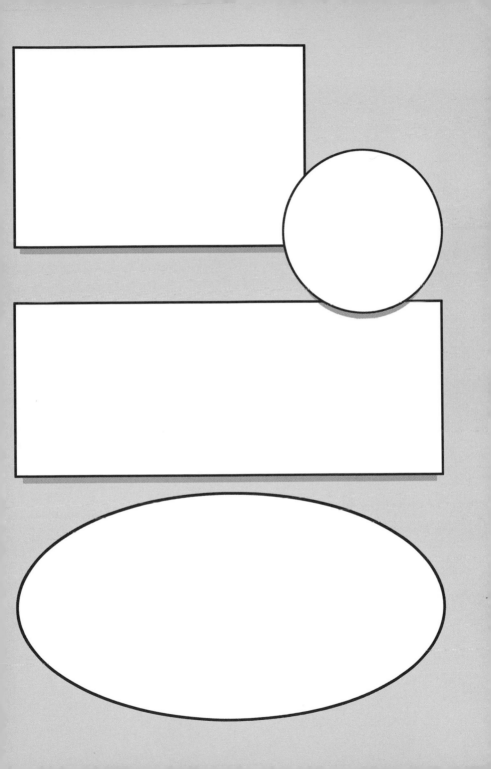

Fun Facts about the Author:

✓ I'm a pescatarian (don't eat meat except fish).

✓ I have freckles in my irises.

✓ I grew up shy and artistic. (Guess who Emmie was based on?)

✓ Although I'm a pescatarian, I sometimes cheat and eat hot dogs. (Hey, I'm human!)